I AM KING

KELSEY GREEN

Cover Design & Editor: Sherelle Green
Proofreader: Cassandra Hutchinson
Interior Design: Kelsey Green

Manufactured and Printed in the United States of America

I AM

KI
NG

POETRY JOURNAL

Acknowledgments

To my sister, Sherelle, for encouraging me to share my poetry with the world. I can say with 100% certainty, this book would not exist without you. You are my biggest supporter and confidant. Thank you for always pushing me to achieve more.

To my parents, Mary and Carl, you are truly two of the most inspiring people I know and the best role models anyone could have. Every positive outlook I have originates from the loving home and upbringing you gave me. I love you both more than words can say.

And last, but not least, to my aunts, Cassandra and Vallerie! Thank you both for being my sounding board, teachers and loudest advocates, lol. I am so blessed to be surrounded by such strong and incredible women.

A collection of poetry written to empower the mind and evoke self-reflection.

IF IMMERSIVE ART COULD BE WRITTEN, THIS IS WHAT IT WOULD SAY...

Table of Contents

POETRY BOOK

MEETS

SELF-HELP JOURNAL

Poetry with a splash of reflection

- The Key to Being King   9
  - Claiming Your Kingdom
    - Call Me King
  - Running an Empire
    - Repetition.
- The Inner King   29
  - Essence of a King
    - I am a Dreamer
  - Even King's Can't Have It All
    - To My Lost Love
  - More Than a Crown
    - More Than a Trophy
  - The Battle Continues
    - Double Edged Sword
- The Effects of a Kingdom   65
  - Decisions and Consequences
    - Mr. Ex Benefits
  - Stay Humble. The War is Still Being Fought
    - Check Your Privilege
- The End of an Empire   85
  - Royalty
    - Satisfying Compromise
  - The Beginning Reflects the End
    - Black Slate

Time for some self-help journaling

- Quotables & Hashtags   108
- Building Your Kingdom Planner   113
- Inspiration Bucket   115
- Self-Care Month   116
- Journaling   120
- Bonus Content   131

The key to being King...

CLAIMING YOUR KINGDOM

In the end, you must love yourself, live for yourself and define yourself. Discovering who you are can reveal a whole new person entirely or shine a light on the person you've always been. Only you can choose whether that is the end or the beginning.

SONG INSPIRATION:

Self Care by Savannah Cristina

CALL ME KING

I live for you.
Like water dripping from the faucet,
moving toward my dwindling cup,
awaiting you to quench my thirst.

Quench,
like the man who held my heart, before
carelessly casting it aside.

I cooked, I cleaned, I played to his male ego,
I taught his kid,
I gave him friends,
I showed him the world.

"Embrace the twists and turns,
the end is just a destination.
The journey is the true vacation."
I taught him that.

I taught him life,
love,
ease.

I taught him big and little things.
I inspired his dreams.

He became a king,
because I called him king.
Huge, big king unmatched by others.
The only guy man enough to open my legs and
release moans like you've never heard.
I open my mouth like the only thing that can
moisten my lips is his huge, thick...
that's what he heard.

He heard his mediocre strokes bring me to places
I could never reach on my own.
He saw his laid-back demeanor calm the spoiled
princess inside of me.
He saw his efforts suppress me, soothe me,
overwhelm me.
He saw his own fucking reflection begin to shine
through me.
He saw himself, in the lies, he placed on me.

On my own,
I was a queen.

Smart... Sexy...
Sassy when I needed to be.
Light of every room.
My own high roller.
With a confidence and energy flowing from me.

But with him...
with him I was a princess.
Spoiled... Entitled...
Desperate when he needed me to be.
Light on his arm.
Eye candy at his high roller table.
With a newfound insecurity and stress taken
from him.

I was intelligent,
just ask those who truly knew me.
Too smart to fall for him,
but I did.

I was beautiful,
just ask those who saw me.
Too pretty to fall for him,
but I did.

I was wild,
just ask those who tried to tame me.
Too free to be chained by him,
but I was.

That man took my world and made it his.
He took my strength and called it his.
He striped my dreams, my accomplishments,
my love of life and drowned it in a sea of his own
making.

I was a queen with a weakness unknowing.
I was a queen who became a goddamn princess.

But that...
that was yesterday.
That was last week,
last month,
last year.
Hell I'm sorry to tell you, but that girl chose a
different path a decade ago.

I don't open myself to anyone who thinks me, no
better than a princess.
I don't give my mind or soul to anyone

undeserving.
I don't sing, smile, touch or even breathe any
mediocrity, others try to push on me.

I am not a princess.
I am not a queen.
I am a motherfucking king if you need a label,
but best believe no matter who comes and goes, I
will always be me.

Flawed, but perfect.
Timid, but strong.
Relaxed, but intense.
The angel and the bitch.
I had one fuck left to give and I'm sorry, I gave it
to him.

But rest assured what has flourished in his
absence is a better friend than before.
A better sister.
A better daughter.
A better woman.

Trust that I love harder, embrace tighter.
Trust that the girl he claimed as his own became
the woman he lost.

Trust that I didn't lose any part of myself in that
relationship, but instead gained the strength to
persevere.
The courage to be myself.
The wisdom to give no fucks, when fuckers don't
deserve it.

Trust that I leap higher, dive deeper and soar
further than I knew possible.
Life is a journey and I live for me.
I am me.
Just ask me.

I am
too intelligent,
too smart,
too wild,
and too me
to ever again lie to myself.

I am
the sun,
the moon,
the earth,
the dirt,

the possibilities are endless, just again ask me.

Call me cocky.
Call me too self-assured.
Call me any name under the sun.
Because he taught me that all the pressures you
might put on me,
and all the words you might use to demean me,
only reveal the hurt and broken pieces of you.

Every stick you throw and every stone you toss
can't break me, because they are not aimed at
me.

I don't judge, because you are not mine to judge.

I encourage.
I support.
And I believe in you, because everything I do to
you is a reflection of how I view me.
And I love me.
I live... for me.

So **call me king.**

Questions

WHAT'S THE LAST NAME OR TITLE SOMEONE ELSE GAVE YOU?

WHAT'S THE LAST NAME OR TITLE YOU GAVE YOURSELF?

HOW DO BOTH NAMES DEFINE YOU?

After Thoughts...

DRAW ~ WRITE ~ EXPRESS HOW YOU FEEL

RUNNING AN EMPIRE

The belief that past mistakes can be rectified is a meaningful credence. However, the knowledge that time is forever moving forward and repeating past mistakes can be harmful is equally important.

Repetition can strengthen the simplest of words. Therefore, we must pay attention to what words, actions and ideas are being strengthened by ourselves and the people around us.

SONG INSPIRATION:

Have Mercy by Eryn Allen Kane

<u>REPETITION.</u>

You can't avoid change.
Change is inevitable.
The world never stops moving.
You get older each year.
Your body changes every day,
and you can't stop it.

You can't avoid pain.
Pain is inevitable.
The world never stops moving.
You get older each year.
Your body changes every day,
and you can't stop it.

You can't avoid sadness.
Sadness is inevitable.
The world never stops moving.
You get older each year.
Your body changes every day,
and you can't stop it.

Does repetition make things stronger or weaker?

If it makes things weaker, then repeating past mistakes won't matter.
Why learn from them, if history is bound to repeat itself?

If repetition makes things weaker, then the job I hate will get easier.
If I go each day, the hold they have on me will lessen.
If I am miserable every hour, it'll miraculously get better.

If repetition makes things weaker, then losing people will eventually get easier.
Rereading the last text message my loved ones sent me won't hurt over time.
Uttering their last words each morning, will mean less and less each day.

But what if repetition makes things stronger?

If it makes things stronger, then losing people will always be hard.
Uttering their last words each morning, will

mean more and more each day.

If repetition makes things stronger, then the job
I hate will only get harder.
If I go each day, the hold they have on me will be
greater.

If repetition makes things stronger, then my
mistakes matter.
I must learn from past errors and do my best not
to repeat them.

I must only repeat things I wish to strengthen.
Like... it's okay to cry.
It's okay to be sad.
It's okay to feel pain.
It's okay to change.

It's okay to feel lost.
It's okay not to have all the answers.
It's okay to be human.
And it's more than okay to be happy.

It's not okay to give in to others demands, when you believe they're wrong.
It's not okay to be selfish.
It's not okay to intentionally hurt others.
It's not okay to give up on your dreams.
It's not okay...
to purposely repeat anything, you don't wish to become.

Are those good statements?
Is what I said okay?
Should I repeat them?

Life is changing.
The world is moving.
You are growing.
And He is waiting.

Give yourself every opportunity you deserve.
Live for those you've lost.
And please, don't cut it short.

Because life is the one thing you can't repeat.
You can't stop it.
There's no **repetition**.

Questions

WHAT IS THE LAST WORD OR ACTION YOU REPEATED?

WOULD YOU BE EXCITED, UPSET OR INDIFFERENT IF THAT WORD OR ACTION GREW STRONGER? WHY?

After Thoughts...

DRAW ~ WRITE ~ EXPRESS HOW YOU FEEL

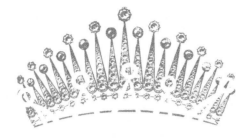

The inner king...

ESSENCE OF A KING

When outside influences try and break who you are then it is important to remember where you come from. Remember the people who make you, you.

SONG INSPIRATION:

Slow Up by Jacob Banks

I AM A DREAMER

When I was a little girl, they would say I lived in
the clouds.
I was a Princess...
No—Queen.
Astronaut...
No—President.
Lawyer and Doctor.
Ballerina.

I was all of them,
one as possible as the next.
Each only a question of _when_ not _if_.
I was a Dreamer.

I put on my grandmother's wig and wailed to
Gladys Knight.
Musician with the sass far beyond my seven
years.
I would be a Guitarist...
No—Lead Singer.
Actress and Model.

The possibilities just grew,
flowing like a never-ending stream.
I was a Dreamer.

Then to school I go, and wonder why each year,
fewer and fewer students look like me.
Why great opportunity seems to send me down a
spiral, where no one here understands me.
The news begins to make sense to me,
as a new color to fear is introduced to me.

We knew hatred was bad before the ones that
hate were able to pull triggers with no
responsibility.

We knew slavery was worse but now they are
erasing it from our history.
Therefore, when we are thrust back there, we are
completely oblivious to its reiteration.

Yeah,
politics make sense to me.
While my eyes twinkle at the 2% on TV.
Being told by the world, that they will never be
me.

Is that reality?
Is that me becoming a...
Realist?

No, no, no,
that's not me.
Time to get home.
Be rejuvenated by their safety.
Grab hold of that security.
Feel my parent's arms around me,
and be reminded that **I am a Dreamer**.

I am an engineer surrounded by people who
don't know me.

I am a traveler retelling myself there are endless
possibilities.

I am a volunteer itching to bring someone up
with me.

I am an author needing to express my creativity.

I am a sister and a friend.
I am a daughter.
A mentor.

This world cannot put chains on me.
My household removed the blindfolds from these
eyes,
and so, each and every time I emerge, I enter this
city with clarity.

Never to be held down by its rigidity.
Never to be numbed by its cruelty.
Never to be duped by its generosity.

Yes, I love this world... and I hate it.
Constantly being reminded that one stray gun
and a barrel of bullets can end it.

But still, I fight the oppression.
I seek all truths and absorb all lessons.
Perpetually reminding myself, that my family
are the reason for all of my blessings.
And they keep me...
as a Dreamer.

Questions

WHAT CHILDHOOD DREAM OR CHARACTERISTIC DO YOU STILL POSSESS?

WHO KNOWS ABOUT THIS DREAM OR CHARACTERISTIC? ARE THEY IMPORTANT TO YOU?

36

EVEN KINGS CAN'T HAVE IT ALL

Discovering what you want, can sometimes take a lifetime; but admitting it, only takes a moment. Sharing your truth is always worth it, if only to yourself.

SONG INSPIRATION:

Another Lifetime by Nao

TO MY LOST LOVE

Love me.
An echo of a wish long forgotten.

I think of it as I watch the Christmas lights
twinkle.
I hear it in the soft breeze off the ocean.
I feel it in the gentle touch against my cheek.

Open your eyes, I'm told.
I do,
but the person staring at me is never right.
The person staring at me is never you.

Sounds cheesy.
Makes you picture a person broken and lonely.
Makes you see someone desperate and deserted.
Makes you paint them brief and unworthy.

Love me.
Simple words...
containing a simple concept...
all built on a simple wish.

Cheesy as it may be,
broken and lonely as it may seem,
desperate and deserted as it's been portrayed,
and brief and unworthy as it has felt.

Time didn't care.
Time didn't waver.

People came and people went.
Future relationships, hitting and leaving as
briskly as the wind that swept them in and then
away.

I listened to the wrong people when it came to
you.

I trusted the wrong thoughts.

"He's not worth it."
"You're too young."
"It can't be real."
The terms flew through the air, ripping us apart.

But none of the voices were yours.

None of the thoughts were mine.

Society tore us apart,
my weakness let you go,
and our life endured it all.

"It's none of your concern!"
I screamed so loud even heaven could hear me,
but I was already too late.

"We're done!"
I yelled at every person who came next,
but it didn't bring you back.

"I choose you..."
I whispered to the past that couldn't be changed.

I'll be waiting in the shade beneath the palm
trees.
I'll sing out when the waves crash against the
shore.
I'll shine bright from the lighthouse that guides
your path home.

Ignore their whispers,
only listen for my voice,
and forgive my past discretions.

Love me...
Let it echo.
Believe in it.
Believe in me.
And come find me, **my lost love**.

Questions

WHEN IS THE LAST TIME YOU ADMITTED SOMETHING TO YOURSELF
THAT YOU WERE NOT READY TO SHARE WITH OTHERS?

WHAT WAS YOUR TRUTH?

After Thoughts...

DRAW ~ WRITE ~ EXPRESS HOW YOU FEEL

MORE THAN A CROWN

Success is measured in many different ways. Being your authentic self may not always line up with the person everyone else perceives.

SONG INSPIRATION:

I Am by Jorja Smith & Kendrick Lamar

MORE THAN A TROPHY

I am more than what they see.
Pretty face and quiet being.
Nice hair and straightened teeth.
Polite girl with simple dreams.

The one you take home to mom, and sure,
company events are a breeze.
For I can impressively hold a conversation, and
be quiet when they speak.

Dates to movies, bars and clubs, somehow always
end the same.
Perfect date, perfect vibing.
It's comical how that never changed.

Perfect curves sounds like a compliment, but it
says nothing about me.
So, I falter for a moment,
overthink and overspeak.
And that hint of caution in their eyes, says
everything I need.

So, cocoon here I come, one more can't handle
me.

I'm the girl inside the woman,
her clumsy, little freak.
I'm the holiday cheer she covers up, when she's
not feeling free.
I'm her ambition and her drive that she
sometimes tucks away when she thinks the world
can't handle all that she has to say.

I'm her dolphin in the water, you can't tear her
from the sea.
That's her happy place she'd love to live, once
she finds her inner fleet.

So, I try and speak,
try and show, all the different sides of me.
But each time it is revealed, that I am more than
what they see.

I am more than the homie,
more than a corporate key.

I am more than a supportive friend,
just take a deeper look at me.

I am more than a sister,
more than a daughter too.
I am more than an apprentice,
to thrive and live your dreams through.

I am more than a college grad,
more than a sounding board.
I am **more than a trophy** wife,
to be put up and adored.

I am not the perfect Barbie that everyone
perceives.
And I am more than an addition to something
already complete.

I am a pessimist,
a realist,
a dreamer and a mess.
I claim all of my attributes, for they've endured
my toughest tests.

Pretty picture I might seem,
but know that in the end,
I am more than I could ever show,
and I know just who I am.

I am *more*.

Questions

A TIME FOR SELF-REFLECTION

WHO SEES ALL THE DIFFERENT SIDES OF YOU? HAVE YOU TOLD
THEM? HAVE YOU THANKED THEM TODAY, FOR LETTING YOU BE
YOURSELF AND NOTICING THAT YOU ARE MORE?

WHAT'S YOUR GREATEST ACCOMPLISHMENT?

WOULD OTHER PEOPLE AGREE?

After Thoughts...

DRAW ~ WRITE ~ EXPRESS HOW YOU FEEL

THE BATTLE CONTINUES

Weaknesses, strengths and insecurities are all in the eye of the beholder. Owning them is an ongoing process which society has come to measure in a term called confidence. The more characteristics you own with confidence, the less power you give other people in using them against you.

SONG INSPIRATION:

Heavy by Kiana Ledé

DOUBLE EDGED SWORD

Just because it's been four months and I haven't
moved on,
doesn't mean I'm weak.

Just because I drunk dialed one man... then
another,
doesn't mean I'm weak.

Just because I scrolled through social media
looking for a distraction or a friend,
doesn't mean I'm weak.

And just because I cried myself to sleep to drown
out my lonely attentions,
doesn't mean I'm weak.

Does it?

The angel on my shoulder answered because she
knows better.
She's smart.

She graduated with honors from a prestigious
university.
She got a six-figure job.
She bought a house.
She's accomplished a lot and she says...
I'm weak.

She wants me to continue working in the field I
earned my degree.
She wants me to remain residing in the city I've
always lived.
She wants me to be secure and place limits on
my risks.
She wants me to get married and have kids with a
stable man.
And she tells me daily that the life she planned
out, is the best life that I can live.

The devil on my other shoulder interjected,
because she doesn't need an invitation.
She's creative.

She never follows a road map because she
believes life will always lead the way.
She wrote a book.
She ran a fashion show.
She's experienced a lot and she says...
I'm weak.

She wants me to push beyond my comfort zone.
She wants me to explore and reside anywhere
that feels different from home.
She wants me to take chances and test my
boundaries.
She wants me to love as many people as I can.
And she tells me daily that the life unplanned, is
the best life that I can live.

When my devil and my angel argue, though,
they sing a different tune.

One defends me for taking four months and not
moving on.
She tells me I'm strong for taking my time and
not to rush my healing.

One defends me for drunk dialing one man...
then another.
She tells me I'm strong for acting on my
impulses, and ignoring others standards.

One defends me for scrolling through social
media looking for a distraction or a friend.
She tells I'm strong for observing the world
through the safety of my phone, before entering
it.

And one defends me for crying myself to sleep to
drown out my lonely thoughts.
She tells I'm strong for releasing the pain of
missing those I've loved and lost.

One of them makes some bad decisions.
One of them has good solutions.
One of them helps me escape dangerous
situations, and one of them drags me into them.

One of them encourages me.
One of them warns me.

Such varied views.
Such different opinions.

By calling one the devil and one the angel, did I
fool you into thinking that one was bad, and one
was good?

Both push me to accomplish things.
Both cause me to pay more attention.
Both are honest, and both are liars.

But most importantly,
both are me.
And occasionally, neither are me.
Occasionally...
Fuck them.
They're just a **double edged sword**.

I'm not just weak,
I'm not just strong.
I'm two sides of one coin.
Two versions of the same incident.

Two chapters of one book.
I'm simply...
A work in progress.

Questions

A TIME FOR SELF-REFLECTION

WHAT WAS THE LAST ACTION YOU TOOK THAT COULD BE
PERCEIVED AS WEAK, OR BROUGHT TO LIGHT ONE OF YOUR
INSECURITIES?

WHAT WAS YOUR LAST ACHIEVEMENT THAT REVEALED YOUR
STRENGTH?

DOUBLE EDGED SWORD

After Thoughts...

DRAW ~ WRITE ~ EXPRESS HOW YOU FEEL

The effects of a
kingdom...

DECISIONS AND CONSEQUENCES

Friendship is love in its simplest form. It can be strong, but when mixed with other feelings and other concepts, you may also discover just how fragile it can be.

You choose what's worth testing that simpler kind of love, and always remember that it takes two to help it prevail.

SONG INSPIRATION:

Imported by Jessie Reyez & 6LACK

MR. EX BENEFITS

I'm sorry my friend, but where is my benefit?
You see that guy lying in the sheets, becomes
more of a stranger each time we meet.
That man I invited into my home resembled a
person I'd known for years, but by the time he
departed my bed he'd twisted into someone else
entirely.

Maybe rhyming would help me describe all that
he became.
Not typical...
but here we go.
Lets describe who he is today.

You see my friend with benefit, you tricked me.
Turned my friend into a foe.
The funny guy who stammered over his words,
became a man I don't care to know.

You see my friend with benefit, you deceived me.

Turned my prince into a toad.
The smart guy I once taught my lessons to,
now pretends he's the brightest bulb.

You see my friend with benefit, you betrayed me.
Turned his respect, temporary.
The nice guy who once shared his most private
dreams,
afterwards placed me on the shelf with many.

You see my friend with benefit, you could have
told me the truth.
That laying with a friend in an intimate setting,
would do nothing to soothe.

It wouldn't soothe my broken heart, broken from
another I left behind.
It wouldn't soothe my loneliness.
It wouldn't leave me satisfied.

It wouldn't soothe so many things, so I'm done.
Do you hear me?
I'm through.

Because my friend with benefit,
you know exactly what I knew.

We were friends first,
and that's where we should have stayed.

Lovers second,
my most positive mistake.

Associates third,
wishing for a better state.

And nothing...
thereafter.
No rhyme to set in place.

Friends with benefits, I'll speak until you hear
me.
Because friends we are no more.
And the only benefit I ever found were
inadequate strokes, when I was feeling low.

Crossing lines, we can't uncross.

Giving in when we needed to be strong.
Damn, I wish I'd known before, how it'd grow to
feel so wrong.

Wish I would have known friendship was love in
its simplest form.
Wish I would have known adding benefits would
change the game long-term.

Wish you would have warned me that I doubled
down, when I was meant to fold.
Wish you would have warned me it's ill-advised,
to replace a hand with cards unknown.

Friends with benefits,
a simple phrase of two words that don't belong.
I warn you not to mix them, and objectively
move along.

Seriously, why'd we do it?
I was over him before we started.
I was never into him the way I wanted.
So, tell me...
why'd I do it?

Did he know I saw another, felt him every time
we touched?
Did he know he stunted my healing?

Yes...
I remember admitting that much.

Did **Mr. Ex Benefits** know I'd feel guilty, no
matter how misplaced?

Damn...
I told him that too.
So, maybe honesty was another mistake?

Admitting I was over him, before we even began.
But I wasn't over us, I wasn't over my friend.

I wasn't over the child who shared his boyish
dreams.
The friend beneath the dick, that now I only see.

I hurt that guy before, pushing him aside more
than once.
And in turn he did the same, putting plenty of
others first.

So alright, my friend with benefits, it's only fair
to let you know,
that before you come knocking,
before I open my door.

Before comfort is confused for pleasure,
blinding my feelings of regret.
Know that I'm over you my friend, the last
benefit will be assuring you that.

The last benefit may not rhyme,
at which task I have failed.
But as long as others heed my warning,
then I feel I've prevailed.

I'm truly sorry my friend with benefit,
I've often wished I could undo, all the lessons
that you taught me, and power that I gave you.

I'm sorry my friend, but where is my benefit?
I guess by now it should be clear,
that the only benefit of screwing you,
was losing something dear.

IF TODAY WAS THE DAY YOU PUT IN THE WORK, TO GET BACK
SOMETHING YOU'VE LOST, THEN WHAT WOULD THAT SOMETHING
BE?

IS IT IN YOUR ABILITY TO FIX?
IF NOT, THEN LET IT GO, THAT'S THE LAST THING LEFT TO DO.
IF SO, THEN WHAT IS HOLDING YOU BACK?

After Thoughts...

DRAW ~ WRITE ~ EXPRESS HOW YOU FEEL

STAY HUMBLE.
THE WAR IS STILL BEING FOUGHT

Blaming others may be temporarily satisfying, but taking responsibility can prove more rewarding.

Checking your privilege is a concept some may need to hear more than others, but the real lesson is in remembering your blessings, especially when society tries to take them away. Stay humble, your work is never done.

SONG INSPIRATION:

Chief Don't Run by Jidenna

CHECK YOUR PRIVILEGE

Little black girl,
check your privilege.

Yes you, with the curly turned straight hair.
Yes you, with the debt turned 401k.
And yes you, with the shared apartment turned
single living condo.

What?
Were you feeling bad for yourself?
Did those men talk down to you again?
Did your skin make them uncomfortable and
force you to set them at ease?
Did you count the seconds until you were free?

You've heard the term white privilege, right?
The state of mind of those who have never been
judged by the color of their skin.
The state of belonging to any place in this
country because they are the majority.
The state of being for those who don't fear the
people in blue, but embrace them for keeping
them safe.

Ah yes,
you've heard of that privilege.
You've witnessed it every day.
Endured it more hours than you can count.
Given into its ignorance and excused yourself
from the table when it reared its ugly head.

Yes,
you've been victimized by its brutality.
Laid off when too many people who looked like
you, but caused less commotion than you,
entered the room.

What?
Did that make you mad?
Are you angry because life isn't fair?
Did that person screaming Affirmative Action
each time you got promoted get you down?
Or did the smile on their face when you were
finally pushed out, piss you off?

If so, then there's only one thing left to do,

Check
Your
Privilege.

I'm sorry, did you think making it in that room
was enough?
Did you think paving the way for others who
look like you, was all you had left to do?
Are you feeling sorry for yourself, that they used
all of that against you?

Yeah, I thought so.
Therefore,
check your privilege.

Those doors that were opened haven't fully shut.
Those barriers that were breaking, are not fully
rebuilt.
Those assholes that were smiling, are not done
spreading their hate.

You are given this one life to live.

Did you hear that?

If not, I will repeat myself because this is important.
You are given this one life to live.

And in the life that your parents, grandparents, great-grandparents and ancestors were given, do you know what they did?
Look around at the things you have.
Look at the places you've gone.
Embrace the freedoms you've been given.
And realize that in that one life they all had to live, they spent it paving this life for you.

They slaved.
They fought.
And they endured,
so that you could flourish.

So, when life gets hard, and you struggle to care, I only have one thing to say to you.
Check. Your. Privilege.

Questions

A TIME FOR SELF-REFLECTION

WHAT ARE YOU MOST ANGRY ABOUT IN YOUR LIFE?

WHAT ARE YOU MOST GRATEFUL FOR IN YOUR LIFE?

WHAT CAN YOU DO TO CHANGE EITHER? AND DO EITHER REQUIRE
YOU TO CHECK YOUR PRIVILEGE?

After Thoughts...

DRAW ~ WRITE ~ EXPRESS HOW YOU FEEL

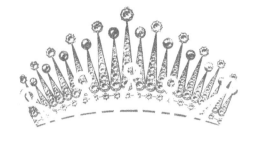

The end of an empire...

ROYALTY

There's nothing wrong with a woman knowing how to love herself, so that she is open to loving the right man.

Mr. Right will embrace your deepest desires as much as you do.

SONG INSPIRATION:

Stay Ready (What A Life) by Jhené Aiko & Flawless

SATISFYING COMPROMISE

Horny Diamond, calm the fuck down,
I don't have time for you today.
Your lustful inclines are way too brash and
stressing me out,
in every
single
way.

I hear you screaming that a release, will quiet all
of your desire.
But girl, you better get a grip!
Today's tasks are not even close to being done.

You already woke me up last night to release
your shameless resolve.
It's only been eight hours since then, so,
seriously...
What the hell is your issue now?

I get my skillful motions no longer impress your
immensely boujé soul.

He ruined you and me incessantly.
Fuck, having any safe word.

But for a lady of my caliber, climax is meant to
be expressed in hushed tones.
So Bitch,
I need you to decompress, before we are both
exposed.

Women can be hornier than men,
is a truth my man should never know.
For admitting to him that secret fact,
can reveal far more than I want to show.

It's a notion that will lose us women all of our
dear clout,
including an ability decades in the making, to
mold men into a well-trained spouse.

Stop pulsing underneath the table, each time our
sexy man enters the room.
He's already ours, and honoring our soul, in and
out of the bedroom.

He's the man of our wet dreams, for far more
than his skillful tongue.
So, it's understandable that you,
my lady parts,
are becoming even harder to control.

I'd say you and I have had a healthy sex drive,
for as long as I recall.
But keeping that lust under wraps was the *first*
lesson of our debutant ball.

Every woman is aware of the secrets we behold.
Taking charge is just another, old story being
told.

Revealing our once hidden assets of confidence
and strength, patience was our biggest virtue.
So, Diamond,
Sis,
figure out your place.

Women's ability to be the smartest in the room,
is a fact we made everyone aware.

But highest sex drive, might be one hundred
times more than men can bare.

So, girlfriend, just think of sports every time our
man is near.
Think of foul balls and bases stolen...
damn,
even that sounds dirty to my yearning ears.

Sure, your horny preceded him,
but love in its realest form,
released the Diamond I now yell at,
who won't be silenced anymore.

Diamonds were said to be a girl's best friend, but
new lessons I have learned.
For when my man and I are making love, equal
appreciation is earned.

You see before he read all my poems, and
attended every speech,
Diamond was less than inclined to give that man,
whatever he needs.

Before he took me to that play, and paid for my
parents too,
she wasn't quite aware how attentive he was,
noticing everything we loved to do.

He cared about the details of my day,
no matter how mundane.
And feelings of love he always expressed,
even in the simplest way.

Therefore, it's no surprise that Diamond
decided, each day has its price.
And if he's not between my legs, then something
just isn't right.

Sure, she loved his tatted six-pack abs, and his
adorable face.
But that heart of his was the main prize, that
earned him her forever place.

So, it looks like Diamond takes the cake,
she's a naughty novice once more.
She taught me that loving the right man, was lust
in its greatest form.

Not a competition to be fought between his sex
drive or mine.
But the perfect combination.
A truly **satisfying compromise**.

Questions

WHAT ARE YOUR DEEPEST DESIRES?

HAVE YOU EVER BEEN WITH SOMEONE WHO NOT ONLY KNEW
YOUR DESIRES, BUT HELPED YOU ACHIEVE THEM?
WERE YOU IN LOVE? AND IF SO, HOW DID IT FEEL?

After Thoughts...

DRAW ~ WRITE ~ EXPRESS HOW YOU FEEL

THE BEGINNING REFLECTS THE END

Strong. Black. Educated. Talented.

We've been told for most of our lives that having these four lethal weapons make us a threat in the eyes of society. No matter our background or upbringing, we aren't born into this world with a clean slate, and must deal with prejudices and discrimination along the way.

However, the adversity we've faced have made us stronger as a culture, and with that knowledge comes blessings, expectations and even hate.

We all have our own experiences. Some may experience less. Some more. No journey is the same, yet we're all connected in our discoveries.

SONG INSPIRATION:

Last Supper by DSmoke (Rythme & Flow)

BLACK SLATE

There is no blank slate when you are born black.
It is not the true color of our skin, and it is the
opposite of our soul.
But somehow, when you are born black in this
country, the slate is never clean.

It's impossible to clear my **black slate**.
It precedes me into the room.
It draws attention before I utter a word, and
screams even when my voice is silenced.

My black slate has immense power, and strikes
fear, from what I'm told.
As though my skin itself can shot bullets, from a
barrel of nothingness.

Like my eyes can strike you down, with one
deathly blow.
And although my muscles barely lift 40 lbs.,
they somehow can threaten a whole armed force.

My black slate, has a reputation.
She is angry at this world.
She is hard to deal with and confrontational,
according to people she doesn't even know.

I also heard she's lazy.
Hard work she often avoids.
She'd prefer a simpler life built of guns, gangs
and ghettos.

Funny thing is, I've never been called loud.
I'm shy to almost everyone I've met.
And I've never been in a fight, therefore, I doubt
I'd be an equal opponent.

I work harder than my counterparts, longer
hours to prove my worth.
But somehow despite my A+ scores, I fail to make
the board.

I'm not part of any gang, and the hood is not my
home.
But I sometimes find it more accepting, than
places where I stick out like a sore thumb.

My black slate, somehow is stronger, than all that
I've accomplished.
My black slate is somehow hated, for things I've
never done.

Some people are born with a blank slate, to be
nourished from the ground up.
Like a sturdy house, they are supported, from
the very start.

Foundations are poured; frames are placed;
and layers are added with careful thought.

The house is assumed to be good, with no
expectations before it's raised up.
A clear mind and a clear heart,
being cherished and rewarded, like some perfect
work of art.

If the house should hold any secrets, then happy
memories are what's assumed.
For the house was built to be home.
Somewhere to be safe and rest once the day is
through.

But my black slate was not like a house, more
like a rundown room.
With dark corners holding fearsome surprises,
of ignorant descent.

The room came with expectations from the
moment it was abandoned.
First impressions were made from images, before
they even stepped inside.

The room was said to hold secrets, of past crimes
and hollowed screams.
The room contained something evil, although it
appeared empty to me.

The room would never clear the essence of
everything it'd never done.
For its impossible to clear a stigma built on
nothing but assumptions.

A concept so deeply imbedded, it possesses
generations to come.
Is there even a point of fighting, when the haters
think they've won?

My black skin may never know the freedom of
invisibility.
Although my voice may often observe, it can be
muted without cause.

My eyes may often see the injustices this world
inflicts.
While my legs may need to grow stronger,
escaping dangers unprovoked.

My hands might wave in the air, every time I'm
pulled over and searched.
But realize my black slate gave me a community,
far stronger than whatever is shown.

My black slate taught me patience, and love in its
greatest form.
My black slate gave me thick skin, and the truest
friends a girl could know.

My black slate gave me my mind, and a pure
soul.
My ability to empathize and endure in an unjust
world.

So, although my slate was never clear, from the
moment I was formed.
I would never trade it for another,
it is the greatest gift I've earned.

IF YOU COULD GO BACK AND WIPE YOUR SLATE CLEAN, WHAT
THINGS WOULD YOU ERASE FROM YOUR HISTORY, IF ANY?

DO THEY STILL HOLD YOU BACK, AND WHY?

WHAT TOOL DO YOU HOLD WITHIN YOURSELF THAT MAKES YOU
POWERFUL BEYOND MEAURE? EXPLAIN IT.

After Thoughts...

DRAW ~ WRITE ~ EXPRESS HOW YOU FEEL

"QUOTABLES"

&

#Hashtags

"I AM A MOTHERF***ING KING IF YOU NEED A LABEL"

#MyOwnKing

"TIME DIDN'T CARE"

#Choose Wisely

"I AM MORE THAN WHAT THEY SEE"

#ByeBye Barbie

"CHECK YOUR PRIVILEGE"

#Humble Practice

"A LADY OF MY CALIBER"

#NoSafe Word

"YOU CAN'T STOP IT"

"A COMPETITION TO BE FOUGHT, BETWEEN HIS SEX DRIVE OR MINE"

"FIGHT THE OPPRESSION"

#SoBeHappy

#Satisfying Compromise

#LiveYour Dreams

"I'M TWO SIDES OF ONE COIN"

"EVERYTHING I DO TO YOU, IS A REFLECTION OF HOW I VIEW ME"

"I'M SORRY MY FRIEND, BUT WHERE IS MY BENEFIT?"

#WorkIn Process

#LoveIsLove

#ScrewYou

"MY BLACK SLATE HAS A REPUTATION"

#F***TheirExpectations

BUILDING YOUR OWN
KINGDOM PLANNER

YOU'VE ALREADY STARTED

YOUR LIFE MILESTONES

DESCRIBE CHALLENGES

CREATE SOLUTIONS FOR EACH

Inspiration Bucket

TOP THINGS THAT INSPIRE YOU

YOUR TOP CAPTURED MOMENTS

TOP WORDS OF WISDOM

SELF-CARE MONTH

- Do A Detox
- Do Some Fun Cardio
- Re-read Your Favorite Book
- Read Something New
- Meditate
- Unplug From Social Media
- Sleep In
- Get A Massage
- Get A Manicure & Pedicure
- Drink A Glass of Wine
- Take A Long Bubble Bath
- Reconnect With An Old Friend
- Have A Girls Night
- Indulge In Your Favorite Dessert
- Bake Something Just For Fun
- Do Something Spiritual
- Create A Piece of Art
- Plan A Weekend Getaway
- Physically Go Shopping
- Get Out & Enjoy A Sunset
- Go To An Art Museum
- Try Two New Activities You've Always Thought About Trying
- Plan Your Perfect Date Night (Take Yourself No Matter What)

NOTES:
ITEMS CAN BE COMPLETED IN ANY ORDER AT YOUR LEISURE

creating art

FIND YOUR CONCEPT:

book

painting

sculpture

music

poem

ACQUIRE REFERENCES:

research

get inspiration

poem

COMPOSITION:

newspaper

chose your material

woodworking

EXECUTION:

physically create

add texture

design

layer your art

PRESENTATION:

show friends

show family

share on social media

travel itinerary

DESTINATION:

DURATION OF STAY:

FLIGHT DEPARTURE:

HOTEL DETAILS:

FLIGHT ARRIVAL:

DAY 1	WHAT TO DO:	BUDGET:
DAY 2	WHAT TO DO:	BUDGET:
DAY 3	WHAT TO DO:	BUDGET:
DAY 4	WHAT TO DO:	BUDGET:

date night

CHOOSE A DATE:

CHOOSE YOUR DREAM
ACTIVITY:

ADD THE APPETIZERS TO
YOUR NIGHT:

BEGINNING	START IN A GREAT HEAD SPACE:	NOTES:
MIDDLE	ENJOY YOUR ACTIVITY:	NOTES:
SOMETHING A LITTLE EXTRA	ENHANCE YOUR EXPERIENCE:	NOTES:
A SWEET END	ALL GREAT THINGS MUST COME TO AN END BUT ENDINGS CAN BE SWEET:	NOTES:

JOURNALING

READ, WATCH, WRITE ...

JOURNALING

SWITCHING LANES AT YOUR LEISURE

JOURNALING

PRIVACY, NOT BARRIERS

JOURNALING

UNLEASH YOUR INNER ROYAL

JOURNALING

DRINK TO CELEBRATE YOU

JOURNALING

SMILING LAUGHTER

JOURNALING

EMBRACING INEVITABLE CHANGE

JOURNALING

EXPLORING YOUR OUTER CULTURE INWARDLY

JOURNALING

ONLY YOU CAN TELL YOUR STORY

JOURNALING

DREAMS RECEIVED
MAKE MORE ROOM

WOULD LOVE TO HEAR FROM YOU!

I hope you enjoyed I Am King!
I love to hear from readers and self-help enthusiasts, therefore, please leave a review, message or email me directly!

Keep turning the page for a few more bonuses :)

THE RENEGADE BID

#BlackExcellence

Cadence Alexander was made for love and luxury. Literally she came from #blackexcellence. Her upperclass parents worked hard to ensure she never had to, but when she bids on the handsome and chiseled, Ace Kathan, at a neighborhood auction, she's in for a rude awakening.

World traveler Ace Kathan is always down for a thrill. So when his G-Ma, Mama Peaches, asks him to explain his date he's happy to explain an extravagant one. But what he has planned will be anything but elegant. Nothing like testing a girls resilience and adaptability by roughing it on his rugged million dollar estate.

Check out an excerpt on the next page

EXCERPT: THE RENEGADE BID

"Ouch! Stop tugging me!" Ivory urged as I pulled her toward the stage.

"Come on, he's almost up," I yelled over my shoulder, keeping my stride.

Ducking under these women's flailing arms and dodging their writhing bodies was beginning to feel ridiculous. A random spectator would surely have thought we were at one of those one-day pop-up shops, instead of a respectable bachelor auction to save Southlake Park.

Ha! *Who am I kidding?* Respectable went out the window along with that cat fight over bachelor number ten. We were officially at a flash sale and men were the merchandise.

"Cadence, seriously! You have dragged me into sweaty armpits, thrust me into innocent bystanders, used me as a human shield against that horrid woman ... and I'm not even going to mention that fiasco from ten minutes ago." She closed her eyes tightly while slowly moving her head from side to side.

Stopping my pursuit, I turned to face her. "I know, Ri, I know," I said, rubbing her arms as she continued to shake her head like she could shake out the memory. "We never have to discuss that again."

"I blame you," Ivory whimpered. Her voice had a slight demonic tone to it. If she hadn't been my best friend since kindergarten, I would have sworn she was possessed. But I'd heard that tone before, and it meant two things. Firstly, she was serious, and if I smiled, laughed, snarked, or moved she would cut me. And secondly, I should watch my back the next couple days.

I opened my mouth to respond, but before I could, my breath caught in my throat as I began to recall the 'incident' in question.

Leaning my forehead against hers, I joined in her gently head shake. She could have a point. Just the memory alone was starting to make me gag a little. "We'll just put that in the lost years box, okay?"

She took a deep breath. As her head slowly shook from no into a yes, so did mine.

"Okay... now, let's move it!" I yelled, returning to my forward stride while still clasping Ivory's hand in mine. I heard what sounded like a grunt come from her direction but I was too focused to care. Ace Kathan was a mysterious enigma that every girl in Chicago wanted to understand. But extraordinary people were not easily figured out by ordinary bunches like everyone else. He needed a woman like me! Not to toot my own horn, because that's just tacky... plus, there's no need since everybody knows who I am and tends to do it for me.

"All right, ladies, next up is Bachelor #19... Mr. Adrenaline Junkie himself."

As the announcer continued to sing Ace Kathan's many praises, my eyes drifted from her to the chiseled man accompanying her onstage. I'd seen him before, I mean obviously since every great men's magazine in the country had published an article on him. His photos always exuded such confidence, mystic ... and most of all, an unwavering sexiness.

"Damn, he's even cuter than I remember."

"What?" I barely heard Ri's question over my own thoughts.

"Oh, you heard that?" I smiled bashfully. "Thought I said that in my head."

Shooting her my infamous 5th grader photo-day look, I refocused on my prize. Bidding had already begun and the vultures were looming.

"$200!" a woman wearing a pink scarf with a red bag screamed. Followed quickly by another bid and another.

"I know. That scarf and bag combo are tragic," Ivory whispered in my ear. I let out a brief chuckle before shaking my head. "Oh I know you noticed!"

Yeah, I did, but it wasn't nearly as bad as the woman in the corner matching her shoes to her lipstick. I mean royal purple, really? I shook the thought from my head.

"And I heard that, too," Ivory giggled.

"I didn't say anything," I murmured, glancing at her.

"Purple?" she questioned with a sly smirk on her lips. "And you say I'm the mean one."

Ugh, that's so creepy! I hated it when she read my mind.

"You don't know that's what I was thinking," I replied. "And you're petty, not mean," I continued, matching her smile. The bid was already up to $500. Not surprising given the reason for this charity bachelor auction. Mama Peaches, the organizer of this whole shin dig, certainly had a way of inspiring people ... and their checkbooks. Plus, Southlake Park was an important part of Chicago that needed preserving. The rundown buildings and community were never going to survive in this thriving city without some major endowments and help. Just the sort of thing my family was known for supporting.

"$6,000!" I screamed much louder than intended. The auction immediately came to a screeching and silent halt. *Did I just say $600 ... or $6,000?*

"Um, bestie ... I know we like to make an entrance," Ivory whispered, "but six grand?" She lightly cleared her throat for emphasis, "are you crazy?"

Guess that answers that question. My eyes grew bigger with each passing second.

"They're all staring," Ivory stated glancing around the room.

"Mhmm. Yep, I can see that."

"They're making me feel dirty." Ivory's voice had gotten slightly louder than before. She began rubbing her left arm, while repeating the words 'very dirty' a few more times.

"Stop it. Stop it!" I urged, returning to a whisper, despite the realization that you could hear a pin drop in the room right now ... meaning they were hearing everything we were saying.

I could literally feel my body temperature rising, under the intense gaze of the crowd. However, unbeknownst to her, Ivory was quickly pulling their unwanted attention. "Make them stop!"

I wanted to make them stop, but I was paralyzed under the glare of one single pair of eyes. Ace Kathan. His piercing, light brown eyes kept me frozen in place. He was a hard man to read. But boy, did every girl want to try. Unlike his brother, Kadaris, who was a staple here in Chicago, Ace had left over a decade ago. He was an extremely successful businessman who turned his love of traveling into a multimillion dollar enterprise. Couldn't say much else was known about him though, besides the unique way he made his fortune.

"Well, I guess you won!" Ivory smiled awkwardly, still rubbing her arms despite nothing being on them.

The sound of the gavel assured me she was correct. More than I'd planned on spending, but I had won my prize, and if my sources were correct, I was in for the most luxurious and lavish date imaginable with one of the world's most eligible bachelors.

THE DESERT NEVER TELLS

Terri Kensington enjoyed a life of secrets and adventure. Thriving on the corrupt nature of the world around her, she used her skills to uncover others lies and build a reputable career as an investigative journalist. Her need for honesty, along with her tendency to find danger, had led to some of the best and worst moments of her life. But when she stumbles upon the mystery of the Desert, she is quickly reminded things are not always what they seem. Sometimes in order to unveil the reality behind the facade, one must dive deeper than intended.

As the Desert and all its secrets closes in around her, every relationship she holds dear is tested in her quest for the truth. Will she be able to work with the strangers she met and find a way back to who she was? Can men and women truly become friends and nothing more? And can any good come from so much deception?

Check out an excerpt on the next page

EXCERPT: THE DESERT NEVER TELLS

Prologue

I never thought it'd end like this. *Twenty-five years old... successful... great friends...* if I could have one more chance, I wouldn't take any of it for granted again. But choices were made, and mine led me here. Trapped in this place, by these walls.

Could he be trusted? I guess no one could, not anymore.

I lived in a world of secrets and lies. Hell, I made a profession out of not only living in that world but unveiling it. Turning corruption into an investigative journalism career, with one of the best rising teams in the world. Dividing and conquering was key, but my team's biggest success was their ability to use social media, public networks and private businesses to pay for our colorful stories. It might have sounded like we dabbled outside the law, but I used every resource to ensure my stories and earnings were legit.

I built my investigative team from nothing to lead my journalism endeavors. Together, we revealed the truth. This universe was full of so much deception, that only the strong, curious and semi-insane people could possibly uncover it. Those types of individuals were me and my crew. So now the question remained, *how did I prove to be the biggest dupe of them all?*

My best friends... my team... my family. They were the entirety of my honest life and stripping me of them had left me here. In an isolation I never saw coming. Secluded from everyone I had known. Every part of my world was infiltrated with the lies and deception I devoted my life to uncovering. I was supposed to be Big Brother, watching the world and revealing its mysteries. I was supposed to keep people honest.

What a joke, right? Nothing about my life was straightforward. Just a pretty fabrication I unconsciously chose to believe in. One of the first things you learned in my line of work was the dangers of getting too close to your subjects. Just like a detective when they are profiling, good investigators needed to understand the ins and outs of their stories. Knowing classified information was not enough. I had to know *How* and *Why* things were the way they appeared.

And it seemed I had failed to ask those questions to myself. *How was I so good at what I did? Why did things come so naturally to me? Who would be drawn to a person like me? What defects would they also need to have? And more importantly, what the hell should I do now?*

ABOUT THE AUTHOR

Kelsey Green is a travel and video enthusiast with a BS in Civil Engineering. However, when she's not wearing her engineer hat, she can be found expressing herself through visual artistry. From event previews and book trailers, to studio staging and styling, Kelsey sees beneath the surface to capture raw beauty and translate her vision through words and filmic innovation.

Kelsey has been journaling since she was a young girl, so she found it only natural to begin penning stories that reflect the emotion only previously portrayed in her videos. She's now a published author and poet, who enjoys depicting life's adventures through romantic storylines and suspenseful plots. Whether her outlet be writing, video editing or constructing, Kelsey finds it therapeutic to show her ideas and thoughts in an expressive and imaginative manner.

For more information:
f @authorkelseygreen
bit.ly/dollhouse67youtube

Keep in touch!
dollhouse67productions@gmail.com

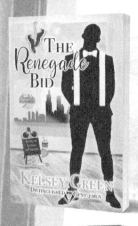

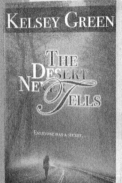

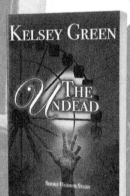

ALSO
BY
KELSEY
GREEN

Printed in Great Britain
by Amazon

26532519R00084